WHY ARE YOU BROKE WHEN YOU SAY YOU KNOW JESUS

Pamela Tucker

WHY ARE YOU BROKE WHEN YOU SAY YOU KNOW JESUS?

Printed in the United States of American

 First printing, 2019

ISBN:978-0-578-63712-9

Email: ReStartenterprise2017@gmail.com

Dedication

First, I thank God for His grace, mercy, and strength to complete this book without God none of this would have been possible.

I thank God for my beautiful family

My daughters Olivia, Antiea, Breanna, and my precious grandbaby Peyton. My siblings Mary, Jimmy, Brenda

Thank you all for your prayers and support, push, and encouragement. I love you all.

To my Leaders Apostle Travis & Pastor Stephanie Jennings

Thank you for your prayers and the prophetic words that keep me moving forward to what God has for me.

I like to extend my heartfelt gratitude to Mr. Jimmy L Tucker (my Brother)

Thank you for inspiring me to write this book and for the title. Thank you for the countless hours we conversed about this one word BROKE!

Table of Contents

Introduction

While I was sitting at the Reading Tea Palace, enjoying a good cup of white cranberry cinnamon tea, I was working on writing a book, but I felt like I could not do it. By this time, I was a little frustrated and it was showing on my face. Sitting there sipping my tea, I noticed a well-dressed older gentleman walking inside. There was something about him. I could not pinpoint it, but I had more important things on my mind. I took a moment and bowed my head to say a quick prayer. Father, if it is meant for me to write this book, send me some help. In Jesus' Name, Amen. When I lifted my head, this man was standing in front of my table.

"I beg your pardon," he said.

I could not help but notice that you were praying about something and a wearisome look is on your face. He looked down at my notebook and said, what a fascinating title. Let me introduce myself.

"My name is Mr. J' Lee," he said. "Hi, my name is Kamille," I replied.

I am just looking like okay, now what? Before I could say anything, he says, may I sit down? I'm thinking no in my head, but my mouth said, "yes, sir, sure!" He sits down and begins to talk. I am listening to him because what he is talking about is what I'm trying to write about.

"Why are you struggling to write this book," he asked?

Before I could answer him, he said, you don't feel you have what it takes to write it, do you?

"That is correct," I replied.

"Do you believe in Jesus?" he asked. "Yes, I do," I responded.

"Then why are you broke?" he asked curiously. Suddenly the story began....

Chapter 1

Broke Excuses

I had a conversation with a group of people, and I asked them this question. Why do you say you're broke?

Listed below are some of the following reasons:

- I haven't got paid yet
- I had to pay some bills
- I'm between blessings
- It's around the corner
- Money is coming to me one day
- Too many children to feed
- Having a financial delay
- They were born broke
- Don't know
- Need a better job
- Need a job
- Can't save any money

- Money doesn't come to them

- Don't have enough money
- It's not for them to have money
- Jesus was broke
- Fear money
- God did not give them money
- Family takes it all
- Money is evil

I just named a few reasons they gave. As you can see, they targeted everything toward money. I was a little surprised by the answers they were giving me because these people say they know Jesus. They were so hyped about talking about their money issues. I allowed the conversation to continue for a moment. I could tell that some of these people didn't know much about money, besides working on getting it and spending it. They never knew how to let the tool of money work for them. So, I begin to tell them about a discussion I had with someone that I think they would be interested in hearing. I begin to share the story with them.

I met a man by the name of Mr. J. Lee, and we had a conversation about being broke. He began to say to me, "to be broken and know Jesus is to have holes in your situation. Don't get broke and poor mixed up. They are different."

I was getting ready to ask him a question, but he suddenly cut me off by saying, "perhaps another time and another book. Now back to the reason why people have holes in their situation. Let me show you an example. Look at this Styrofoam cup." He put a tiny hole in it and poured some water in. Mr. J'Lee begins to say that this is how some people's situation is at times. They have a tiny drip in their finances while other people may have multiple drips because of the poor decisions they have made. They knew it was wrong, but they did nothing to correct it. Some people are being chased by the giant of debt that calls out:

"Fee-Fi-Fo-Fum, I smell the blood of the broke one."

When he stopped talking, it was quiet for a few minutes. Then, I asked a question. "Mr. J'Lee, "what makes a person not try and fix the drip or drips in their finances?" "Because some have been like that for a while, and others were raised to think about money differently. For some people, it's hard to change their way of thinking. If they are still doing, seeing, and speaking the same thing over their life, they will continue to get the same outcome."

I understood what Mr. J'Lee was talking about.

"Sometimes people don't ever detox their minds from negative thinking about things they don't understand like money, he said wisely. So, let us keep going to the question on the table."

Why Are You Broke And You Say You Know Jesus?

So, we jumped right into the conversation again. He said, "Why do you think people say they are broke?" I said, "The reason I believe some people are broke and say they know Jesus is because of FEAR!"

"Fear, hmm?"

"Yes, people fear a lot of things, like birds, snakes, crowds, heights, being alone, making decisions, and so much more, but one more thing would also be money. Some people are broke because they have a fear of getting money or even losing money, paying bills with money, etc. They stress out over money, needing it, wanting it and don't know how to handle it. Some people have Chrematophobia (intense fear of money)."

Mr. J'Lee said most people are leaning and submitting to their thinking. They never get to the point to say enough is enough and ask God why they are broke or why are my thoughts like this about money; even my actions toward money? Some people don't even pick up a bible to read what God has said to them about money. They believe what was told to them when they were growing up and hearing some parents and even pastors say that money is evil. Money is not evil. But it's the love of money that's rooted in all kinds of evil.

Let us read the whole scripture about what God said about the love of money.

1 Timothy 6:10 {NIV} For the love of money is a root of all kinds of evil. Some people, eager for money, have wandered from the faith and pierced themselves with many griefs.

Mr.J'Lee proceeded, "let us read a couple more scriptures so that when money comes to us because it will come, that we will not be arrogant nor put our hope in it. It is to help others and for our enjoyment. We put our hope in God.

1 Timothy 6:17 {NIV}

Command those who are rich in this present world not to be arrogant nor to put their hope in wealth, which is so uncertain, but their hope in God, who richly provides us with everything for our enjoyment.

2 Corinthians 9:8 {NLT}

And God will generously provide all you need. Then you will always have everything you need and plenty left over to share with others.

I shared with the group to be careful about what they think, don't allow negative thoughts to enter your mind. Also, don't speak what you see speak what you desire, speak what God says you can have.

I encourage you all to pray about what we have shared with you all and understand that being broke is not always money.

2 Timothy 2:7 {ESV}

Think over what I say, for the Lord will give you understanding in everything.

Matthew 6:31-33 {NIV}

So do not worry, saying, 'What shall we eat?' or 'What shall we drink?' or 'What shall we wear?' For the pagans run after all these things, and your heavenly Father knows that you need them. But seek first his kingdom and his righteousness, and all these things will be given to you as well.

Chapter 2

Broke Mind

The mind is powerful. We have to be watchful about what we think. The Bible speaks about how powerful the mind and our thoughts are. Some people's thoughts have been contaminated by negativity, not only in their thinking but in their speaking. All of this goes hand in hand. Your thinking has a lot to do with your speaking. What are you thinking that is causing you to speak the wrong thing? Do you know that your thoughts help create who you are? That's why it is so important to think about yourself the way God thinks about you. Let us read what he said in his word.

Jeremiah 29:11 {NIV}

For I know the plans I have for you," declares the Lord, plans to prosper you and not to harm you. Plans to give you hope and a future.

God has extraordinary thoughts about you. Why are you thinking something different for yourself? Understand what wrong thinking does for you. If you think you are, you will be what you think, and what you think, you now speak, and what you speak you now see. Let's read what God says about what you think.

Proverbs 4:23 {EEV}

Be careful how you think. Your thoughts make you the person that you are.

Change the way you think, and your speaking will change. Then what you see will change as well. Think Positive, Hope, Love, Forgiveness, Joy, Peace, etc.,

Choose to think greater for your life. Again, I say if God is thinking exceptional thoughts about you, why not think the same for yourself? God has great plans for you. Someone may ask how can I do that? How can I think the same way God thinks about me? First, you have to want God to transform your broken mind, broken thinking and broken speaking. We can find the answer in the word of God.

Romans 12:2 {NLT}

Don't copy the behavior and customs of this world, but let God transform you into a new person by changing the way you think. Then you will learn to know God's will for you, which is good and pleasing and perfect.

You have to change your negative thinking about your life and everything that is attached to it. Your mind is very powerful, delete meaningless stuff from your mind.

Philippians 4:6-8 {NLT}

6 Don't worry about anything; instead, pray about everything. Tell God what you need and thank him for all he has done. 7 Then you will experience God's peace, which exceeds anything we can understand. His peace will guard your hearts and minds as you live in Christ Jesus.

8 And now, dear brothers and sisters, one final thing. Fix your thoughts on what is true, and honorable, and right, and pure, and lovely, and admirable. Think about things that are excellent and worthy of praise.

Chapter 3

Broke Hand

Mr.J'Lee and I met again at a tea and pastry shop. We always had the best conversation, no matter what topic we were talking about.

So, he comes in and says, "hello' Kamille, how are you?" I replied, "I am great! How are you, Mr. J'Lee?"

"I am supercalifragilisticexpialidocious," he said with a big grin. "Oh wow, that's a mouth full," I said.

He said, "Kamille, I want to tell you a story. On the way here, God told me to share this with you."

"Okay, I hear you," I said.

"I need you to not only hear me, but I need you to listen to me," he replied. Unsure of what he would say, I said, "let us pray first. I don't want to miss what God wants me to know from your story."

So, we prayed. Once we were finished, we said Amen, and he began to tell this story. Mr. J'Lee told me a story about a young boy. One day, this boy came home from school. He would always go straight to the refrigerator when he got home. This young boy was a little pudgy and liked to eat. So, this particular day, he goes to the refrigerator, and there was no food in it. The young boy was very upset, and he spoke out of his mouth, one day I will eat whatever I want, when I want and closed the refrigerator. What this young boy didn't know what he said was coming to pass. This boy spoke with such faith at 11 years old, he begins to save pennies and he starts a paper route. He started to work in other places, and by the time he turned 23, he had money and businesses. He had everything he spoke that day and more. He could eat whatever he wanted, whenever he wanted. He got a lot of materialistic things, but not the right way. He was heading down the wrong path.

Thankfully, this boy had a praying mother that tried to warn him to straighten up and do right. She began to tell him that God had something great planned for his life. He would not listen, even though he told his mom, alright! Ok, I will change, which was a fabrication; not long after that, he went to jail. When he went before the judge, the prosecutor read off over 30 charges and asked for him to be sentenced for one year in jail per charge. The other people in the courtroom were whispering among themselves, saying this young man is going away for a long time. The Judge called for a 15-minute recess. The young man's oldest sister Sarah was in the courtroom, so she went out to call their mother and told her it was not looking good for him. Their mother was silent, and then she says, "not so! That's not what God said." She begins to pray and

Thank God for a turnaround. His sister Sarah went back into the courtroom. They were getting ready to restart the hearing, so the defense attorney tried to speak on behalf of the young man. However, all the evidence said that he was guilty. The Judge stops the defense Attorney in his speech and asked the young man to stand up. The Judge repeats all the charges, and the evidence says you are guilty. However, it's something about you. The Judge said I am ready to rule. Charge 1 dropped. Charges 2 dropped. Charges 3 dropped. The judge went down the list calling out over 30 charges and dismissed over half of them, and then he says, you are sentenced to 3 years in prison. Everyone was at awe with unbelief that the young man had got such a low sentence. When the young man got to the prison, after being there for a few days, he had to go before the prison board, not knowing what they would say. He thought they were going to add time to his sentence. When he arrived, they said, "young man, somebody must be praying for you. Your file has come to our attention, and we are not sure why, but we looked at your case, and we decided to drop 2 more years from your sentence." The young man was amazed. He thought about what his mom said in a conversation days ago to him. Begin to Thank God for the favor He has placed on your life. He realized that God had given him favor with man. He was very grateful to God. His mom would come every Sunday to see him and share the word of God with him. When I told her what God had done she rejoiced in that place.

He said, "What man thought should have been 30 years. God said, ``not so!"

Mr. J' Lee said that this young man did 8 months, 18 days, 9hours and 36 minutes with only a few seconds in prison. While he was in prison, God used him to start a bible study with over 75 attendees, including some of the guards. He was also placed over the prison warehouse, where all the meat comes to feed the prison staff and inmates. When this young man got out of prison, his shero came and picked him up and took him shopping for a pair of pants and shirts to go to church and to find a job. The young man remembers what a couple told him when you get out of prison. You have a job with us. So, the young man went to see Mr./Mrs. Coleman about a job. Mr. Coleman was very thrilled to see the young man. He said I have a job for you, cutting, cleaning and wrapping, fish.

The young man became the fastest fish cutter in his county. Mr. J'Lee said that this man is now the owner of several investment properties. He is an owner of restaurants and grocery stores. He is a business visionary, a philanthropist. He is a husband and a dad, as well as a Pastor.

I said, "Mr. J'Lee, so who is this man that has this amazing testimony?"

He smirked a little and said, "That's his testimony. Because of his role model, he started going to church and accepted the Lord Jesus Christ as his Savior, and he got baptized, and GOD filled him with the Holy Ghost."

I said, "What an amazing testimony. I asked who was his shero/role model?"

He said, "His mother was his Wonder Woman. She was my shero," he said with tears in his eyes. When he was a baby, she would say: *"You're my pride, you're my joy, you're my big ole baby boy.* I loved her so much! I told you my story because I want you to know that no matter where you are in your walk with Christ, God can and will use you if you surrender your all to Him.

God has placed greatness in your hands."

He said his life could have made another turn besides prison. I could have gotten out with the same mindset, still doing the same thing, acting the same way, hanging with the same crowd and ended up dead. Thank God for a praying mother that would not give up on her children. My mother told me I have to make a choice. Either you are using your gift for good are you are using it for evil.

Mr. J' Lee said he knew what gifts he had in his hand, but he made a bad choice when he was younger. He said I used my gift for (evil) to get me fast money and other things. I did this for years. My mother kept giving me warnings, but I did not listen. He said when he spoke to his team, he would ask, who has God put in your life to let you know that you are going the wrong way or are making the wrong choice?

He said after a while, his choices got him in some deep trouble. My mother asked me to read this.

Deuteronomy 30:19 {NIV}

This day I call the heavens and the earth as witnesses against you that I have set before you life and death, blessings and curses. Now choose life, so that you and your children may live:

"Thank God for another chance to make the right choice. I had to choose life. I made up my mind to allow God to work on and in me to do want he has called me to be!" Mr. J'Lee said he speaks to people every day, and he tells them to make a wise choice Life or Death. He said, "then I asked them what's in your hands?" Then he gave some scriptures.

Exodus 4:2 {NIV}

Then the LORD said to him, What is in your hand?"

What gifts has God placed in your hands that you are not using? Or you are using for evil and not for God.

God has given us all a gift/s, what are you doing with what God has given you? Use your gifts that God has given you to help others.

Romans 12:6 {NIV}

We have different gifts according to the grace given to each of us.

Mr. J'Lee said, Kamille, "do you have anything you would like to add to this conversation?"

Yes, sir, I do. I would like to ask a question to someone who is feeling useless who has broken your hands from using the gifts that God has given you? We don't all have the same gifts, but what is it that you should be doing that you are not doing. Understand that what's in your hand is not for you. Some people are waiting for you to sing, teach, preach, cut meat, start a business, write the play, feed a stranger. etc. What's in your hand that will change someone's life?

If you started using what's in your hand at one point in you life,but stopped along the way for whatever reason, I want to encourage you to restart again.

Remember what Moses had in his hand, a rod. God used what Moses had in his hand to perform many miracles, and it set many people free. What will God do with what's in your hand when you are giving it to Him?

Psalm 90:17 {NIV}

May the favor of the LORD our God rest on us; establish the work of our hands for us yes, establish the work of our hands.

Chapter 4

Broken Relationship

Mr. J'Lee and I wanted to talk a little about different Broken Relationships, Family, Friendship, Divorce, Health, Death. You may have experienced one if not all in your life, at some point that it has caused you to become broken.

However, we will not talk about any of those, but I would like to ask you a question. How is your relationship with Jesus?

So many people have a broken relationship with Jesus but won't admit it. How is your relationship with Jesus?

Do you know him because of your parents, your role model, or do you know him because your pastor knows Him? How do you know Jesus?

People might say that they know Jesus, as a healer, helper, a way maker, protector, etc. If that's all you know about him you have a limited relationship with Jesus when HE is so much more....

You know Jesus in a religious way when you only speak to him when you have a problem for him to solve, or when you have gone to everyone else, and

23

they can't help you, then you come to Jesus. You have a religious relationship. Jesus should be your go-to first and foremost.

If you want this kind of relationship with Jesus, you have to drop all your guards. You must make up in your mind that you what to know Jesus intimately.

Understand this is not talking about a one-night stand, but this is talking about an intimate relationship with Jesus; a deep, commitment closeness, conversation, communication taking time to spend with Jesus listening and praying beginning still in his presence in this time it's just you and Jesus...

Jesus said that he no longer calls you a servant, but He calls you a friend. Jesus loves you so much that he died for you.

John 15:15 {NIV}

I no longer call you servants, because a servant does not know his master's business. Instead, I have called you friends, for everything that I learned from my Father I have made known to you.

Romans 5:8 {NIV}

But God demonstrates his own love for us in this: while we were still sinners, Christ died for us.

You cannot have a one-sided friendship with Jesus. It will lead to a stagnant relationship, not on Jesus' part, but your part. Jesus will never stop loving you. Make a choice.

Let us look at the story about Martha and Mary.

Luke 10:38-42 {NIV}

38. As Jesus and his disciples were on their way, he came to a village where a woman named Martha opened her home to him. 39. She had a sister called Mary, who sat at the Lord's feet listening to what he said. 40. But Martha was distracted by all the preparations that had to be made. She came to him and asked, "Lord, don't you care that my sister has left me to do the work by myself? Tell her to help me!"

41. "Martha, Martha," the Lord answered, "you are worried and upset about many things, 42. But few things are needed—or indeed only one[a] Mary has chosen what is better, and it will not be taken away from her."

Ephesians 5:15-16 {NIV}

Be very careful, then how you live - not as unwise but as wise, making the most of every opportunity because the days are evil.

They both had a relationship with Jesus. Martha had a religious relationship, but Mary had an intimate relationship with Him.

I ask you again what type of relationship do you have with Jesus?

I remember when I was growing up, I used to hear the mothers including my mom in the church sing a song that says, Just a closer walk with thee. Theses saints of God wanted an intimate relationship with Jesus.

I encourage you to ask GOD to search your heart and if HE finds anything that hinders you from walking close and even having an intimate relationship with Jesus,to take it out of you and replace what needs to be.

Chapter 5

Broken Finances

One day Mr. J'Lee and I opened up our discussion about money to a group of people that love Jesus, but they said they were broke financially.

Everyone had their own opinion about their reasons for being financially broke.

They were given different reasons one person said that money was rarely talked about in his home when he was growing up, Another said that she was only told that money is to pay your bills and take care of your family.

They all were told something different concerning money.

Then this man named Josiah said that money was a very touchy conversation in his home as a boy. As he grew up, he heard people say that money is a tool and make your money grow for you. He said that his dad would tell him money doesn't grow on trees.

Josiah said when they went to church, the preacher would say now we are at a time where we all can take part; now dig deep and give God what belongs to Him.

Josiah said, "I never understood that either. Don't everything belong to God?" Josiah, at his age of 27 years, said it's so much: I don't know about money but wish I did.

Mr. J'Lee asked Josiah, "Do you read your Bible?" He replied, "Sometimes." Mr. J'Lee asked, "do you know that God wants you to have money?" Josiah said he was told that money was evil by his dad and the preacher when he was growing up.

Mr. J'Lee said, "You need to change your thinking. You are a man now; you have to put what was told to you as a child away." Let us read…

1 Corinthians 13:11 {KJV}

"When I was a child, I spoke as a child; I understood as a child, I thought as a child: but when I became a man, I put away childish things.

Mr. J'Lee said you have to understand some things that were told to you as a child was incorrect. Now that you are an adult, you can acquire the knowledge to know the truth about what was told to you that you may gain an understanding for yourself.

Mr. J'Lee asks the group, how many are members of a church, out of the 12, only 3 say they were members? Some of the others said that they visit sometimes, they said the church has changed. "How so?" asked Mr. J'Lee. Someone replied, "I don't get nothing out of it." Mr. J'Lee, "hmm, what are you putting in it. You can't get anything from nothing. If you what something out of it, you have to put something into it. He went on to say, do you go expecting God to speak to you?

Mr. J'Lee said you all are wondering why you are financially broke. I will not ask who pays tithes and offering, but I will say this is an area in your life you need to take notice of. I would also suggest to those that don't go to church to get in a bible teaching church that believes in the Lord Jesus Christ. Pray and ask God to open up your understanding not only your finances but your understanding of who God is in your life."

Luke 24:45 {NIV}

Then he opened their minds so they could understand the scriptures.

Mr. J'Lee said God owns everything, including you.

Psalm 24:1 {KJV}

The earth is the Lord's, and the fulness thereof, the world, and they that dwell therein.

Mr. J'Lee said, "do you have anything to add, Kamille?" Yes, I do. Do you all know that money, wealth, possession is mentioned over 2,300 times in the bible? Do you ever wonder why?

This is just my opinion, but could it be because Jesus knew such a thing could be the downfall of men and women of today? Jesus knew it would be the very thing that would draw people away from God.

Some people do a lot of bad things to get money,

Some people's money has become their god.

Could it be that your money has become your god?

Some people trust their money more than they trust God.

They feel like their money can do everything for them, so with that thinking, they don't need God. WOW! How does one forget who blessed them with the wealth/ money?

Deuteronomy 8:18 {ESV}

You shall remember the LORD your God, for it is He who gives you the power to get wealth, that he may confirm his covenant that he swore to your fathers, as it is this day.

We have to trust God in every area of our life. He will never leave us; it is nothing that we go through or need that God does not see, hear, and even know.

I truly understand about being broke financially, but I have come to find out that if you would put Jesus first in everything you do, he will make a way for you. So, ask for more than money. Ask for the knowledge of money because money will surely come, but what you do with it counts. Who will you help? Who or what will you give to? How will you help?

Understand that you can't serve your money, but you can use your money to serve God. Here are a few scriptures to think about.

Matthew 6:24 {NIV}

"No one can serve two masters. Either you will hate the one and love the other, or you will be devoted to the one and despise the other. You cannot serve both God and money.

Matthew 6:21 {NIV}

For where your treasure is, there your heart will be also.

That's all I will say for now. The group was all into the discussion. One of the ladies in the group said she is going to read her Bible not just about finances, but how to serve God in everything. Some said they needed to put Jesus back in their life. They were all excited, confessing, repenting and asking God for forgiveness, even Josiah said he prayed and asked God to lead him to a Bible-believing church, that he may learn more about God.

Mr. J'Lee said that he would like to add one more scripture

John 8:32 {NIV}

Then you will know the truth, and the truth will set you free".

Chapter 6

Broken To Better

Weeks have gone by since I had spoken to Mr. J'Lee. My mind was still playing the conversations we had in the discussion group almost a month ago. I reminisce about the reasons they were giving for being broke. They started out talking about money, but I was talking about life.

I had a meeting coming up with another group of people.

When I met them, my question was, Why Are You Broke When You Say You Know Jesus? I am not just talking about money. I am talking about life.

They call out different areas in their lives they were tired of being broke in such as

- Heart
- Mind
- Spirit
- Finances
- Health

Why Are You Broke When You Say You Know Jesus?

- Marriage
- Family
- Relationships
- Job
- Business
- Friendship
- Church
- Faith
- Love
- Belief
- Debt
- Prayer

After listening to them talk about the different areas of their lives of being broken. I realize that their brokenness brought something out of them they don't seem to recognize. Once they were finished talking, it was silence for a moment

I said let me ask a question most of y'all said that heartbreak was a part of your brokenness in your life they all said yes; I said despite your brokenness you were able to give love to someone else and still giving it.

What I'm saying is look at your brokenness it helped you to become who you are. You know how it feels to be broken so you learned how to give compassion, encouragement and so much more because of your experience with brokenness.

Don't allow your brokenness to make you bitter but let it make you BETTER.

Chapter 7

Broken Limits

As the group and I continue to we spoke a little about broken limits.

We have a Savior that loves us, and HE wants us to trust and believe that HE will deliver us out of whatever we are in, no matter how we feel or what we think.

However, we can delay what God wants to do for us and through us, by putting limits on Him. You can limit God to your thinking and even your speaking.

You have to take the limits off God, I would say break the limits off. God is so much more than want we think.

I know you heard the story of Jabez. He did not allow what his mother called him to stop him from wanting greater for himself. He took the limits off he's speaking and asked God for something incredible.

1 Chronicles 4: 9-10 {NIV}

Jabez was more honorable than his brothers. His mother had named him Jabez,[a] *saying, "I gave birth to him in pain." Jabez cried out to the God of Israel, "Oh, that you would bless me and enlarge my territory! Let your hand be with me, and keeps me from harm so that I will be free from pain." And God granted his request.*

Why are you afraid to ask God for something unimaginably?

Could it be that you don't believe HE will do it for you?

Mark 11:24 {NIV}

24. Therefore I tell you, whatever you ask for in prayer, believe that you have received it, and it will be yours.

Take God out of the box of boundaries.

God can do all things but fail. Do you believe that?

If you doubt God to answer your prayers, you have limits on God. Take God out of the tiny box just to pay your bills.

Could it be that being broke in whatever area of your life is because you have limits on God and trying to do things on your strength?

You have to believe that God can, and God will answer you.

Take the limitation off your prayers, thinking, and even your speaking.

- What are you speaking over yourself?
- What do you think about yourself?

Why Are You Broke When You Say You Know Jesus?

- What are your prayers for yourself?

Take The Limits Off of God Pray, Believe, and Receive.

We serve a limitless GOD!!!

Because you are someone's pride and joy, and they are waiting for you to make a choice. It's time for you to surrender all to God and walk on Faith Highway; no longer are you stuck on Fear Court. You can have everything God said you can have if you ask HIM and **ONLY BELIEVE**.

Confessions

- I am not Broke
- I am Better
- I am Blessed
- I am getting all my needs met by Jesus
- I am healed by the stripes of Jesus Christ
- I am forgiven
- I am a giver
- I am wealthy
- I am helping others and myself
- I am a new creature
- I am not defeated
- I am walking by faith and not by sight
- I am walking in victory
- I am not alone
- I am the righteousness of God in Christ Jesus
- I am in the company of good friends
- I am more than a conqueror
- I am the head and not the tail

Why Are You Broke When You Say You Know Jesus?

- I am a lender and not a borrower
- I am blessed in the city
- I am blessed in the fields
- I am a child of God
- I am redeemed from the curse of the law
- I am walking in Supernatural abundance
- I am free from debt
- I am living in limitless favor
- I am a child of an infinite GOD

Be honest with yourself.

Could it be you have not cast all your cares on Jesus?

Could it be that you don't believe HE can do it?

Could it be you have limits on God?

Could it be that you are speaking negative words over your life?

Take some time and ask Jesus why are you broke in any area of your life then write the answers

This is not to say that you will not go through any brokenness at some point in your life its how you deal with the brokenness when it comes.

Be Healed and Whole In Jesus' name.

Beautifully Broken

To be broken is like having no hope and the feeling of being lost unloved to live in a world of doubt and unbelief, the place of fear a sense of not knowing where to turn and who to turn too.

You wonder how can you move forward when you're feeling stuck unsure about the what, who, where and why's in your life.

I realize that if I had never been broken, I would have not known about the gifts that God has given me. In my brokenness, I learned forgiveness, repentance, encouragement, prayer, compassion, kindness, Love and so much more.

My relationship with Jesus changed for the Better.

Being broken may not feel good, but I understand its part of the process.

I Believe God allows the brokenness for us to see the gifts he has placed in us.

Don't allow your brokenness to make you bitter but let make you Better.

Pamela Tucker

Prayer

Father God, In the name of Jesus, I pray for those who are feeling broken in any area of their life.

I know that these feelings can be intolerable. I pray that the peace of God exceeds every broken area of their life. I pray that they will not be held back by their brokenness, but they will bounce back in balance and the BLESSINGS of the LORD as they lean and depend upon your words. I pray they obey what you have instructed them to do and to be in this world.

In Jesus Name, Amen.

About the Author

Pamela Tucker is an advocate for the forgotten.

Her heart for people and effort to help others live their best life has made her an active humanitarian. She has three daughters and one granddaughter.

Pamela is the author of the books Forgive Me Forgive Me Not Vols 1 & 2.

Pamela resides in Metro- Atlanta where she continues to live a life of Forgiveness.

Why Are You Broke When You Say You Know Jesus?

www.ingramcontent.com/pod-product-compliance
Lightning Source LLC
Chambersburg PA
CBHW021916040426
42447CB00007B/886